Creature Comparisons

Comparing Creatures

Rupert Fandangleman

www.raintreepublishers.co.uk
Visit our website to find out more information about Raintree books.

To order:
☎ Phone 0845 6044371
🖹 Fax +44 (0) 1865 312263
🖥 Email myorders@capstonepub.co.uk

Customers from outside the UK please telephone +44 1865 312262

Raintree is an imprint of Capstone Global Library Limited, a company incorporated in England and Wales having its registered office at 7 Pilgrim Street, London, EC4V 6LB – Registered company number: 6695582

Text © Capstone Global Library Limited 2009
First published in hardback in 2009
First published in paperback in 2010

Edited by Rebecca Rissman, Siân Smith, and Charlotte Guillain
Designed by Kimberly Miracle and Joanna Malivoire
Picture research by Tracy Cummins
Originated by Capstone Global Library
Printed and bound in China by Leo Paper Products Ltd

ISBN 978 0 431 19427 1 (hardback)
13 12 11 10 09
10 9 8 7 6 5 4 3 2 1

ISBN 978 0 431 19431 8 (paperback)
14 13 12 11 10
10 9 8 7 6 5 4 3 2 1

British Library Cataloguing in Publication Data
Fandangleman, Rupert.
  Comparing creatures. -- (Acorn plus)
  1. Animals--Variation--Juvenile literature.
  I. Title II. Series
  591.4-dc22

Acknowledgements
The author and publishers are grateful to the following for permission to reproduce copyright material: Age Fotostock p.**8 left** (© Tier und Naturfotografie/J&C Sohns); Alamy pp.**6** (© Verge Images/Tom Soucek), **17 middle** (© David Fleetham); Getty Images pp.**7 left** (© Visuals Unlimited/Brandon Cole), **8 middle** (© Tim Laman), **15 right** (© The Image Bank/David Tipling), **21 right** (© Photographer's Choice RR/Bo Tornvig); Photolibrary pp.**5** (© Digital Vision), **11 right** (© Digital Vision/Martin Harvey), **17 left** (© Mark Webster), **17 right** (© Photographer's Choice/Kevin Schafer), **19 left** (© Photodisc/Michael Aw); Shutterstock pp.**4** (© Shane Wilson Link), **7 middle** (© FloridaStock), **7 right** (© IBI), **8 right** (© Zaporozhchenko Yury), **9 left** (© Keith Levit), **10** (© John Bell), **11 left** (© Nick Poling), **12** (© Tom C. Amon), **13 left** (© Tom Grundy), **13 right** (© Nicola Vernizzi), **14** (© Marilyn Barbone), **15 left** (© Boris Z.), **15 middle** (© rick thornton), **16** (© Andrey Parfyonov), **18 bottom left** (© Pakhnyushcha), **18 bottom right** (© ethylalkohol), **18 top left** (© Zdorov Kirill Vladimirovich), **18 top right** (© Alvaro Pantoja), **19 right** (© Karel Broǐ), **20 left** (© John A. Anderson), **20 right** (© Stefan Glebowski), **21 left** (© Drahomir Kalina), **22 top left** (© Shane Wilson Link), **22 top middle** (© John Bell), **22 top right** (© Tom C. Amon), **22 bottom left** (© Marilyn Barbone), **22 bottom right** (© Andrey Parfyonov).

Front cover photographs reproduced with permission of Photolibrary: bird (© Corbis), frog (© Creatas), monkey (© Tim Laman), bear (© Radius Images), and Shutterstock: fish (© Geanina Bechea), snake (© John Bell). Back cover photographs reproduced with permission of Shutterstock: elephant (© IBI), starfish (© Alvaro Pantoja).

We would like to thank Nancy Harris and Adriana Scalise for their help in the preparation of this book.

Every effort has been made to contact copyright holders of any material reproduced in this book. Any omissions will be rectified in subsequent printings if notice is given to the publisher.

Contents

Some words are shown in bold, **like this**. They are explained in "Words to know" on page 23.

Animal groups

There are different types, or groups, of animals. Animals that are in the same group are similar.

Animals in the same group share **characteristics**. But they can look or act very differently, too.

Mammals

backbone

Mammals are animals that have fur or hair on their bodies. Mammals have **backbones**. All baby mammals get milk from their mothers.

There are many different types of mammals.
Mammals live all around the world.

Monkeys are a type of **mammal**. But not all monkeys are alike. Some monkeys run. Some monkeys leap. Some monkeys swim.

Bears are a type of mammal. But not all bears are alike. Some bears have white fur. Some bears have black and yellow fur.

Reptiles

backbone

Reptiles are animals that are covered with **scales**. Reptiles have **backbones**.

Snakes are a type of reptile. But not all snakes are alike. Some snakes swim. Some snakes slither.

Amphibians

backbone

Amphibians are animals that can live in water or on land. Amphibians have damp skin. Amphibians have backbones.

Frogs are a type of amphibian. But not all frogs are alike. Some frogs use **camouflage** to hide. Some frogs have bright skin. Some frogs have poison in their skin.

Birds

backbone

Birds are animals that have feathers. Birds have **backbones**. They have two wings and two feet. Birds have a beak. Birds hatch from eggs.

Not all birds are alike. Some birds fly high in the air. Some birds swim. Some birds slide!

Fish

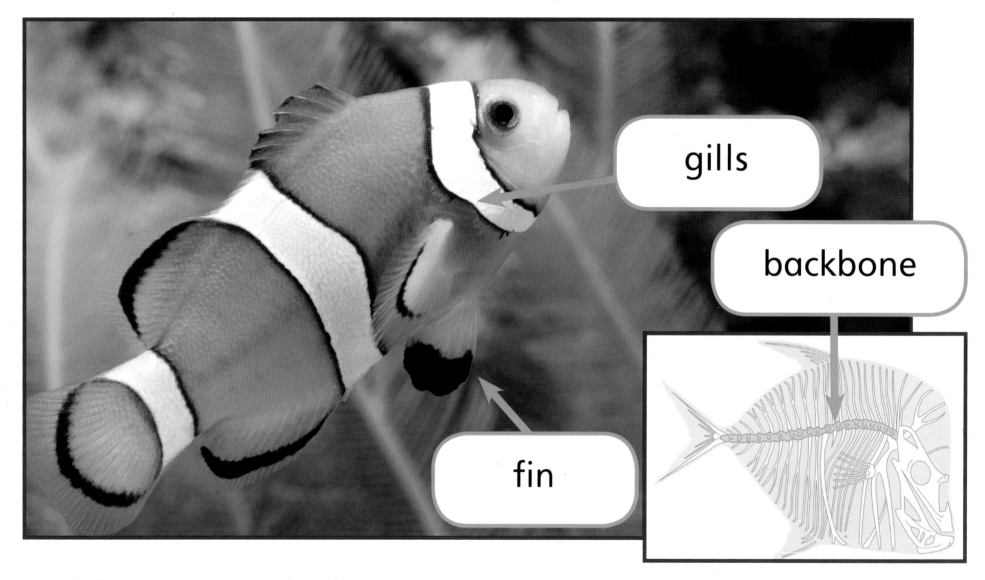

gills

backbone

fin

Fish are animals that live in water. Fish have **backbones**. Fish breathe through **gills**. They swim using **fins** and a tail. Most fish have **scales** on their bodies.

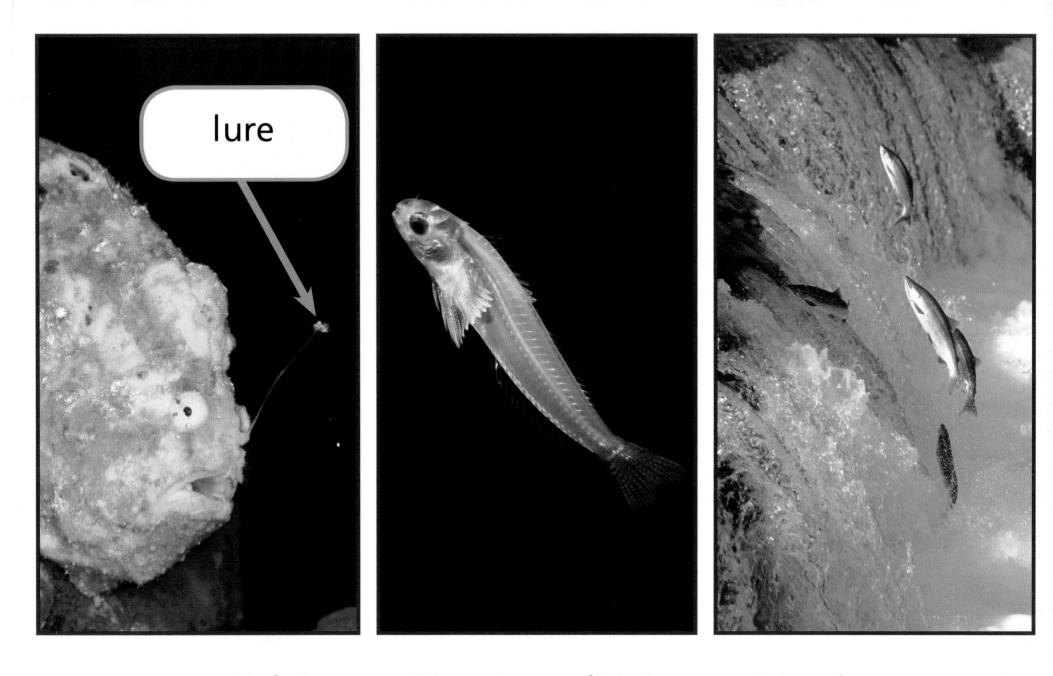

But not all fish are alike. Some fish hunt with a **lure**.
Some fish are **transparent**. Some fish even jump out
of the water!

Animals without backbones

starfish

lobster

worm

spider

Not all animals have **backbones**. The animals in these pictures do not have backbones.

Animals without backbones live around the world.
Animals without backbones can look very different.

Why are animals different?

Animals are different around the world. Some animals are **camouflaged** to hide from other animals. Some animals are brightly coloured to scare other animals away.

Some animals have tails to help them climb. Some animals have tails to help them swim. The different ways animals look and act are important. Animal differences help them to stay alive.

Types of animal

mammal

reptile

amphibian

bird

fish

Words to know

amphibian	type of animal that can live in water or on land
backbone	row of bones that makes up an animal's back
bird	type of animal that hatches from an egg, has a backbone, feathers, two wings, two feet, and a beak
camouflage	cover or disguise that helps something blend in with its background and makes it hard to see
characteristic	the things about a creature or object that make it what it is, for example, how it looks or acts
fin	a part of a fish that helps it move through water
fish	type of animal that lives in water and has a backbone, fins, and a tail. Most fish are covered in scales.
gill	a part of a fish that helps it breathe
lure	something used to tempt creatures to move towards it
mammal	type of animal that gets milk from its mother when it is a baby, has a backbone, and has fur or hair on its body
reptile	type of animal covered with scales that has a backbone
scale	a small, flat plate that covers an animal's skin
transparent	clear or see-through

Index

Notes for parents and teachers

Before reading

Tell the children there are different groups of animals. Animals in the same group have similar characteristics. Some groups of animals are called mammals, reptiles, amphibians, birds, and fish. These groups are similar because they have backbones. Tell children that there are animals without backbones. Hold up pictures of animals with backbones and animals without backbones. Ask children if they can name some of the differences between the animals with backbones and the animals without backbones? What makes these animals special?

After reading

• Tell children that the animals in the book shared similar and different characteristics. Ask if they can remember something special about the mammals? Reptiles? Amphibians? Fish? Birds? Animals with no backbones? Ask children to talk to a partner about which animal group is their favourite.

• Children can create their own picture book of their favourite group of animals. Their books can have descriptions of their animals and/or pictures with a label. When the children have created their books, they can share their stories in small groups or as a whole class.